Noa: A Story of Courage

Jasmine Lawi

Dedication

To my daughters, Noa and Raya

Noa: A Story of Courage

Once upon a time, in a kingdom far away, lived a courageous girl named Noa.

Noa had four sisters: Mahlah, Hoglah, Milcah, and Tirzah.

Noa and her sisters admired their father, Zelophehad.

He was courageous.

Long ago, Zelophehad was born as a Hebrew slave of King Pharoah in the Land of Egypt.

The Hebrew slaves called themselves "Israelites."

One day, Zelophehad gathered his courage, and he boldly marched out of Egypt with the Israelites and their leader, Moses.

The powerful Egyptian army charged after Zelophehad and the Israelites at the Red Sea.

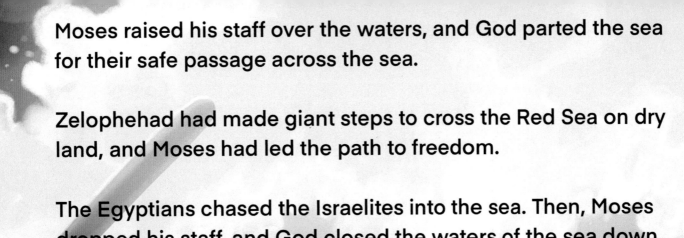

Moses raised his staff over the waters, and God parted the sea for their safe passage across the sea.

Zelophehad had made giant steps to cross the Red Sea on dry land, and Moses had led the path to freedom.

The Egyptians chased the Israelites into the sea. Then, Moses dropped his staff, and God closed the waters of the sea down onto Pharoah's army.

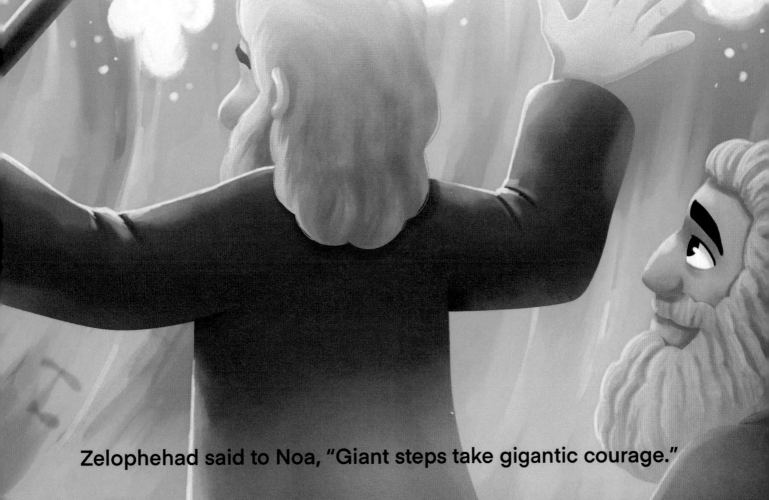

Zelophehad said to Noa, "Giant steps take gigantic courage."

Moses had promised to Zelophehad a purple castle in the new Land of Israel. The purple castle sat atop a green hill.

The hen hatched the eggs. The woodpecker tweeted the tunes. The llama spun the wool to make a warm bed. The turtle slowed down the time. The flying swans whipped up a breeze. The deer gathered the wood to build a fire. The bunny picked the fruit. The puppy barked at danger, and the hungry ponies mowed the grass and trimmed the weeds.

The animals built for Zelophehad a purple castle on his promised land.

Moses and the Israelites had roamed in the desert for ages before the Israelites set foot upon the new Land of Israel.

One terrible night in the wilderness of the desert, Zelophehad wrestled a wild beast with hungry fangs, a prickly nose, a fiery tongue, and a poisonous bite in a terrible dream.

Zelophehad whipped a marble stone from his slingshot directly onto its head, and the wild beast fell back on a bed of thorns. The wild beast yelped again, and painstakingly freed itself, its body trembling with fear.

Zelophehad had fought a great fight. Yet, the might of the wild beast was different, and Zelophehad never opened his eyes again after his terrible dream had ended.

Noa and her sisters bid farewell to their father. Then, Zelophehad ascended to God and the angels in Heaven.

Noa's uncles were terribly evil. They terribly wanted to take Zelophehad's purple castle from Noa and her sisters for themselves.

Noa gathered her courage, and she boldly marched out of her tent with her sisters to speak with their leader, Moses.

The evil uncles charged after Noa at the entrance of the Tabernacle of Moses-a sacred place where God spoke to Moses.

Noa said to Moses, "The purple castle rightfully belongs to my sisters and me." The evil uncles challenged Noa's plea and screamed at Moses, "Only men can own castles!"

Moses was stuck between a rock and a hard place. He gazed up at the blue skies, and he asked for God's help.

God spoke to Moses and said, "The purple castle rightfully belongs to Noa and her sisters." Then, God created a new law that gave women the right to inherit their own castles from their fathers due to Noa's courage.

Noa had made giant steps to defy her evil uncles and to speak with Moses face to face, and God had honored her courage.

The evil uncles aimed their terrible slingshots right at Noa's heart, and they snarled under their terrible breaths, "This means war!"

Noa remained stoic like she had ice water in her veins! Then, God hurled down a ball of fire from his burning bush at Mount Sinai that spun into a ring around the evil uncles.

Noa said to the Israelites, "Giant steps take gigantic courage."

The Israelites entered the new Land of Israel.

Noa played her flute, and her sisters twirled beneath the moonlight and the stars of their purple castle that sat atop a green hill in the new Land of Israel.

The castle animals hymned in harmony, and white doves flocked in a heart-shaped circle since this was their way of dancing in the new Land of Israel.

A Moment to Reflect

What lessons do you think Noa learned from her father, Zelophehad?

Why do you think Moses had presented Noa's and her sisters' case to God instead of deciding it himself?

Do you admire Noa for her courage?

What does "courage" mean to you?

Do you remember a time when you or someone else were scared? What steps did you or they take to feel safe?

Have you ever been treated unfairly?
If so, did you stand up for yourself and how?

What are you most grateful for, and how will you protect it?

What lessons have you learned from Noa?

How do you decide when to act brave and when it is okay to do nothing?

What are your dreams and goals, and how will you achieve them?

How can you become a trailblazer to create positive change in the world?

Made in the USA
Las Vegas, NV
07 March 2024

86775321R00019